THE ULTIMATE ANIMAL LIBRARY

Parrots

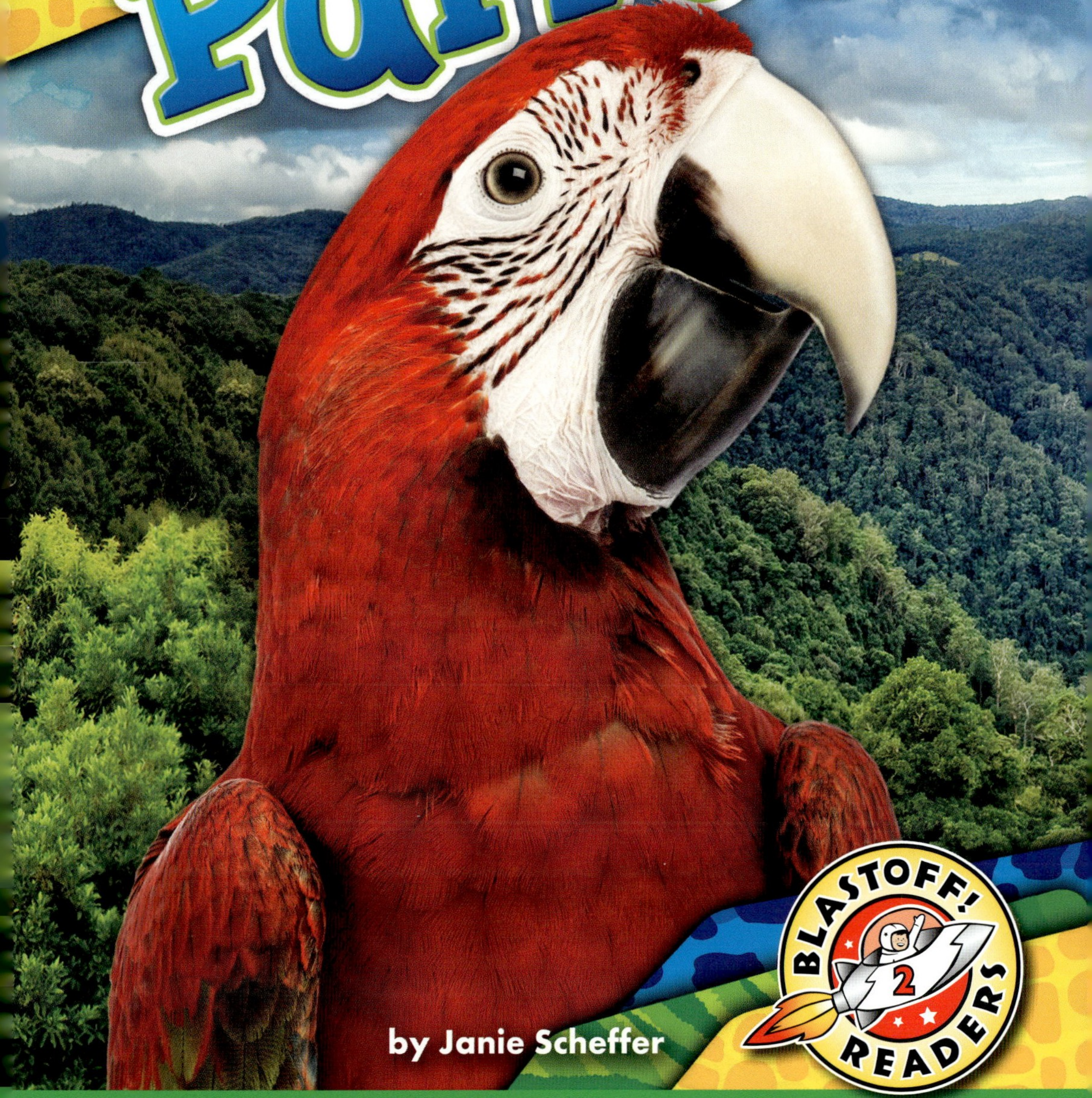

by Janie Scheffer

BLASTOFF! READERS 2

BLASTOFF! READERS, AN IMPRINT OF BELLWETHER MEDIA BY FLUTTERBEE

Blastoff! Readers are carefully developed by literacy experts to build reading stamina and move students toward fluency by combining standards-based content with developmentally appropriate text.

LEVELS

Level 1 provides the most support through repetition of high-frequency words, light text, predictable sentence patterns, and strong visual support.

Level 2 offers early readers a bit more challenge through varied sentences, increased text load, and text-supportive special features.

Level 3 advances early-fluent readers toward fluency through increased text load, less reliance on photos, advancing concepts, longer sentences, and more complex special features.

★ **Blastoff! Universe**

Reading Level

Blastoff! Beginners — Grade K

Blastoff! Readers — Grades 1–3

Blastoff! Discovery — Grade 4

This edition first published in 2027 by Bellwether Media, Inc.

Library of Congress Cataloging-in-Publication Data

Names: Scheffer, Janie, 1992- author
Title: Parrots / by Janie Scheffer.
Description: Minneapolis, Minnesota : Bellwether Media, Inc., 2027. | Series: Ultimate animal library | Includes bibliographical references and index. | Audience: Ages 5-8 | Audience: Grades 2-3 | Summary: "Relevant images match informative text in this introduction to parrots. Intended for students in kindergarten through third grade"-- Provided by publisher.
Identifiers: LCCN 2026013882 (print) | LCCN 2026013883 (ebook) | ISBN 9798898800420 (library binding) | ISBN 9798898801663 (ebook)
Subjects: LCSH: Parrots
Classification: LCC QL696.P7 S335 2027 (print) | LCC QL696.P7 (ebook)
LC record available at https://lccn.loc.gov/2026013882
LC ebook record available at https://lccn.loc.gov/2026013883

Editor: Elizabeth Neuenfeldt Designer: Brittany McIntosh

Printed in the United States of America, North Mankato, MN.

Table of Contents

What Are Parrots?

Parrots are birds. There are hundreds of parrot **species** around the world! Most parrots live in **tropical** areas.

Scarlet Macaw Report

Range

Status in the Wild

least concern

Habitats

forests

savannas

rainforests

Hyacinth macaws are the tallest parrots. They can be over 3 feet (1 meter) tall.

hyacinth macaw

Buff-faced pygmy parrots are the shortest. They are around 3 inches (8 centimeters) tall.

Most parrots have colorful feathers. Others are gray, white, or black.

Parrots have thick **beaks**. Their **curved** shape helps parrots break open nuts and seeds.

Parrots have **zygodactyl** feet. Each foot has four toes.

Two of their toes point forward. The other two toes point backward.

Spot a Parrot

Big Flocks!

Most parrots live in tropical forests. Some live in **savannas**.

Parrots nest in trees, cacti, and groups of rocks.

Most parrots live in **flocks**. Some flocks have up to 1,000 parrots!

Flocks keep them safe
from **predators**.

Parrots are **omnivores**. They mostly eat fruits, nuts, and seeds. They sometimes eat **insects**.

Most find food in the morning and evening.

Growing Up

Female parrots lay one to seven eggs at a time. Both parents **protect** the eggs.

Many take turns sitting on the eggs. After about one month, the eggs **hatch**.

Chicks keep their eyes closed for two weeks. Soon their adult feathers grow.

Chicks stay with their parents for up to two years. They can live for around 50 years!

Life of a Parrot

Name of Babies

chicks

Number of Babies

1 to 7

Time Spent with Parents

up to 2 years

Life Span

around 50 years

Glossary

beaks—the mouths of birds

chicks—baby parrots

curved—bent

flocks—groups of parrots

hatch—to break open

insects—small animals with six legs and bodies divided into three parts

omnivores—animals that eat both plants and animals

predators—animals that hunt other animals for food

protect—to keep safe

savannas—flat grasslands with few trees

species—kinds of an animal

tropical—related to places that are hot and wet

zygodactyl—related to animals that have the toes of each foot arranged in pairs

To Learn More

AT THE LIBRARY

Klepeis, Alicia Z. *Parrots*. Minneapolis, Minn.: Jump!, 2022.

Murray, Julie. *Princess Parrot*. Minneapolis, Minn.: Abdo Kids, 2025.

Thompson, Kim. *Baby Parrots*. Mankato, Minn.: Creative Education and Creative Paperbacks, 2026.

ON THE WEB

FACTSURFER

Factsurfer.com gives you a safe, fun way to find more information.

1. Go to www.factsurfer.com.
2. Enter "parrots" into the search box and click 🔍.
3. Select your book cover to see a list of related content.

Index

The images in this book are reproduced through the courtesy of: Eric Isselee, front cover (parrot); Taras Vyshnya, front cover (background), pp. 2-3; Passakorn Umpornmaha, pp. 3, 11; Alfredo Maiquez, p. 4; SATRIA NANGISAN, p. 6; Gabbro/ Alamy Stock Photo, p. 7; Ian Fox, p. 8; Noppe Herlinde, p. 9; Christian Musat, p. 10; Lennon Geba, pp. 10-11; bilalwebdesigner, p. 12; Danny Ye, p. 13; Tarcisio Schnaider, p. 14; Rafael Martos Martins, p. 15; Reto Buehler, pp. 16-17; Wirestock Creators, p. 17 (eagle); JLugonStudio, p. 17 (jaguar); David Havel, p. 17 (parrot); Leo botanist, p. 17 (fruit); T. Schmidt, p. 17 (nut); Fernando, p. 17 (seed); dreii, p. 18; DLeng, pp. 18-19; Scorpii, p. 20; CHUCHAT TREEPRAPHAKORN, p. 21; ManoStudioArt, p. 23.